Collins · *do brilliantly!*

2005Test**Practice**

KS3English

Test practice at its **best**

- **Alan Coleby**
- **Kate Frost**
- **Series Editor: Jayne de Courcy**

William Collins' dream of knowledge for all began with the publication of his first book in 1819. A self-educated mill worker, he not only enriched millions of lives, but also founded a flourishing publishing house. Today, staying true to this spirit, Collins books are packed with inspiration, innovation and practical expertise. They place you at the centre of a world of possibility and give you exactly what you need to explore it.

Collins. Do more.

Published by Collins
An imprint of HarperCollinsPublishers
77–85 Fulham Palace Road
Hammersmith
London
W6 8JB

Browse the complete Collins catalogue at
www.collinseducation.com

© HarperCollins*Publishers* Limited 2005

First published 2005

10 9 8 7 6 5 4 3 2 1

ISBN 0 00 719500 1

Alan Coleby and Kate Frost assert the moral right to be identified as the authors of this work.

British Library Cataloguing in Publication Data
A catalogue record for this publication is available from the British Library.

Acknowledgements
The extracts in the Reading Paper are reproduced from the following sources: *Tiger Woods* by Jack Clary (Tiger Books International, 1997); 'Through the tunnel' by Doris Lessing, in *Short Stories of Our Time*, ed. Douglas R. Barnes (Thomas Nelson and Sons, 1984); *Biology for Life* by M.B.V. Roberts (Thomas Nelson and Sons, 1981).
Photographs
Lew Long/CORBIS (p. 1); Tony Roberts/CORBIS (p. 2); Roy Morsch/CORBIS (p. 20).

Every effort has been made to contact the holders of copyright material, but if any have been inadvertently overlooked, the Publishers will be pleased to make the necessary arrangements at the first opportunity.

Edited by Jenny Draine
Production by Katie Butler
Design by Bob Vickers
Printed and bound by Martins the Printers, Berwick upon Tweed

You might also like to visit
www.harpercollins.co.uk
The book lover's website

Contents

When is the Test?

You will sit your English National Test in May of Year 9. Your teacher will give you the exact dates.

What does the Test cover?

The English curriculum is divided into three Attainment Targets:

En 1   Speaking and Listening
En 2   Reading
En 3   Writing

The Test covers Reading and Writing. It also covers the Shakespeare play you have studied in Year 9. Your teacher will have chosen one play out of a list of three, and there are two scenes in your play which you will have studied in great detail.

How many papers are there?

There are **three** Test papers:

- The Reading Paper, which is 1 hour 15 minutes.
- The Writing Paper, which is 1 hour 15 minutes.
- The Shakespeare Paper, which is 45 minutes.

Reading Paper

There are three reading passages, with questions in a separate booklet.

The passages are likely to be:

- a passage of prose which is non-fiction (it does not tell a story); it could be a biography or an autobiography, a leaflet, a newspaper article, a diary, a travel book, a magazine article, a letter or an advertisement

- a passage from a novel, short story or a poem

- another passage from any non-fiction book such as a textbook or an instruction manual.

You are allowed 15 minutes to read the three passages and 1 hour to write your answers.

This paper carries 32 marks.

Writing Paper

This paper has two tasks. The first is the **Longer Task**. You are advised to spend 45 minutes on this task, including using the Planning page, which will be opposite the page which tells you what the Longer Task is. You may be asked to write a story, or other form of narrative, where you can be as imaginative as you like, and you can control much of the form in which you write. This is called an 'open' task.

This task carries 30 marks.

The second is the **Shorter Task**. You will have 30 minutes to spend on it, if you have taken 45 minutes on the Longer Task. The task will be a 'closed' or 'directed writing' task such as a letter, a newspaper report or a speech. Information will be provided for you to use in your writing. There is no Planning page for this task.

This task carries 20 marks.

Shakespeare Paper

There is **one task** on this paper about the Shakespeare play that you have studied. You have 45 minutes to answer it, including reading time.

Three plays are set each year. Two scenes from each play are for detailed study, and your teacher will have told you which these are. In 2005, these scenes are:

Henry V	Act 4 Scene 1 Lines 83–202
	Act 5 Scene 2 Lines 98–227
Macbeth	Act 3 Scene 1 Line 74 to end and Act 3 Scene 2
	Act 3 Scene 4 The whole scene
Much Ado About Nothing	Act 1 Scene 1 Lines 119–215
	Act 2 Scene 3 Line 81 to the end of the scene

There are passages from each scene printed on the question paper, and so you do not need to take a copy of the play into the Test.

This task carries 18 marks.

All students sit the same Test papers, and in English there is only one 'tier' resulting in the award of a level from 3 to 7.

v

How to do well in your Test

What is in this book

This book contains:

- complete Test Papers: Reading Paper, Writing Paper, Shakespeare Paper
- the Shakespeare plays and scenes for 2005
- detailed answers and marking guidance.

How to tackle the Reading Paper

You are given 15 minutes to read the three reading passages before you are allowed to write your answers. Make the best use of this time by reading all three passages thoroughly. Start thinking about the language, structure, purpose and audience of each passage. You won't see the actual questions until the 15 minutes' reading time is up, but you can begin to notice key features of the passages which may be of help when you do come to answer the questions.

The questions sometimes advise you to refer to words and phrases from the passage to support the ideas you write about in your answers. This means that you should give quotations from the passage. Quotations are words and phrases or whole sentences copied from the passage. You must remember to put inverted commas in front of and after the words you copy.

There are two things to remember about using a quotation. First, do not make it too long, usually no longer than a sentence. Second, do not just pick out any phrase or sentence, but make it refer to the ideas that you have expressed in your own words in your answer.

Remember that when examiners mark answers to the questions, they do not mark writing style – spelling, punctuation, grammar or paragraphing. They are concerned only with how well you have understood each passage and how relevant your answer is to the question.

Look hard at the mark allocation for each question as this will give you a guide as to how much to write. Spend longer on questions worth the most marks.

How to tackle the Writing Paper

You will be marked on 'Composition and effect' – how interesting what you write is, how appropriate the style you have chosen to write in is, and how well your writing engages the interest of your reader through your choice of vocabulary, etc.

You will also be marked on how well you express yourself: 'Sentence structure and punctuation' and 'Text structure and organisation'.

For the Longer Task, make sure that you use the planning sheet to plan your answer paragraph by paragraph. This planning is not wasted time as it will allow you to write your story more quickly. It will also ensure that your story is carefully constructed with a powerful opening and ending.

Allow at least five minutes to check through your writing when you have finished. Don't worry if you want to change a word – for example, you may want to change an adjective for a more powerful one or add inverted commas around speech. Do any crossings out as neatly as possible and you will not be penalised for this. In fact, you will be awarded higher marks if your editing of your writing has improved it – even if there are some crossings out.

How to tackle the Shakespeare Paper

On this paper there are two passages of about 50 or 60 lines each, selected from the two scenes that have been prescribed for detailed study. There may be a description of the context of the passages. There is then one task written in bold type, which refers to both passages.

You have 45 minutes to read the task and write your answer.

Tasks on the Shakespeare plays are usually of two types. The first is a 'critical discussion' question which will ask you about aspects of plot, character, meaning or language in the scenes. The second is an 'empathetic' question which will ask you to imagine that you are one of the characters and to write as if you were that person.

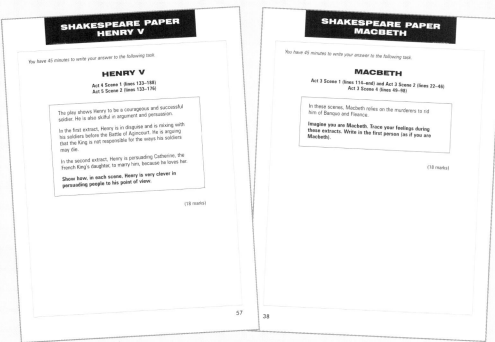

SHAKESPEARE PAPER
HENRY V

You have 45 minutes to write your answer to the following task.

HENRY V

Act 4 Scene 1 (lines 133–188)
Act 5 Scene 2 (lines 133–176)

The play shows Henry to be a courageous and successful soldier. He is also skilful in argument and persuasion.

In the first extract, Henry is in disguise and is mixing with his soldiers before the Battle of Agincourt. He is arguing that the King is not responsible for the ways his soldiers may die.

In the second extract, Henry is persuading Catherine, the French King's daughter, to marry him, because he loves her.

Show how, in each scene, Henry is very clever in persuading people to his point of view.

(18 marks)

57

SHAKESPEARE PAPER
MACBETH

You have 45 minutes to write your answer to the following task.

MACBETH

Act 3 Scene 1 (lines 114–end) and Act 3 Scene 2 (lines 22–46)
Act 3 Scene 4 (lines 49–98)

In these scenes, Macbeth relies on the murderers to rid him of Banquo and Fleance.

Imagine you are Macbeth. Trace your feelings during these extracts. Write in the first person (as if you are Macbeth).

(18 marks)

38

1 A 'critical discussion' question will ask you about aspects of plot, character, meaning or language in the scene.

2 An 'empathetic' question will ask you to imagine that you are one of the characters and to write as if you are that person.

The first of these types of question, 'critical discussion', is the most frequently set. Remember that, in your answer to such a question, you must include quotations. Do not make these quotations too long (two or three lines at the most), and make them refer clearly to the ideas you express in your own words.

With the second of these types of question, it is important to show that you know what all the other characters think, do and say, as well as concentrating on your particular character.

How to work out your marks and calculate your level

Reading Paper

Add up the marks that you have achieved across all the questions on all three passages.

Writing Paper

For the Longer task, award yourself a mark within one of the mark ranges (see pages 23–30 for more details), after reading all the guidance and sample extracts.

Then do the same for the Shorter task using pages 31–36.

Shakespeare Paper

For whichever play you have chosen, decide which mark range your answer best fits, using the guidance and sample extracts provided. Then award yourself a mark within the range (see pages 43, 52 and 60 for more details).

The first table below gives the marks and levels for each paper. The second table gives your level for the three papers together, based on your total mark.

For technical reasons, the thresholds in the real tests for 2005 may be well below the overall thresholds given here.

Level	Reading	Writing Longer Task	Writing Shorter Task	Shakespeare
N	1–5	1–2	1–2	1–2
4	6–12	3–9	3–8	3–6
5	13–19	10–16	9–14	7–10
6	20–25	17–23	15–19	11–14
7	26–32	24–30	20	15–18

Level	Overall marks
3	4–14
4	15–38
5	39–62
6	63–84
7	85–100

Energy for life

Reading Paper

On the following pages you will find three reading texts:

1 An extract from the biography of the American golfer, Tiger Woods.

2 The conclusion of a short story by Doris Lessing.

3 *Getting Energy from Food*, an extract from a Science textbook.

Remember

- You have 15 minutes to read these texts.

- During this time you must not write or open the Answer booklet.

- At the end of 15 minutes you will have 1 hour to answer the questions.

This extract is from the biography of the young American golfer, Tiger Woods.

Without a doubt, Tiger Woods is the result of his father's plan to raise a golf champion. Earl Woods was a good athlete, whose principal claim to athletic achievement was as a baseball catcher during a short time at Kansas State University. Woods was a career Army man who worked his way through the

5 ranks to the rank of lieutenant colonel when he fought in Vietnam. It was during his time in South East Asia that he met and married his second wife, Kultilda Punsawad. Six years later, their only son, Elrick, was born in Long Beach, California, on December 30, 1975.

Earl Woods had big plans for his new son, and they mostly revolved around the

10 game of golf, to which Earl had been introduced a few years earlier. Earl has said that he was driven by the fact that as a black, he had long been denied access to the country-club world of golf. 'But I told myself that somehow my son would get a chance to play golf early in life.' So before Tiger was even one year old, his father would take him out to the garage and put him in his high chair or playpen, where

15 the boy would watch his father pound ball after ball into a practice net and putt ball after ball into a cup.

His father has said that when Tiger was just ten months old, he took up a putter and gave a perfect display of the delicate art of putting a golf ball. When he was three, he won a pitch, putt and drive competition against ten- and eleven-year-olds.

20 But his father didn't limit his instruction to the sheer mechanics of golf. During his years as a Green Beret, he had learned a great deal about shaping a mind to cope with stress, and so he set out to mould his son's mind so that he could master the all-important skill of concentration. At age six, while Tiger was out in his family's garage hitting balls into the same net he had watched his father use, he

was also listening to subliminal messages on a tape recorder. His father had also
tacked messages of positive reinforcement to Tiger's desk in his room. Earl
Woods used a mixture of distractions that could cause a golfer's game to fall
apart. His father did everything, from making caustic remarks before Tiger was
set to tee off or sink a putt, to making noise at the top of his backswing. In Earl's
own words, he pulled 'every nasty, dirty, ungodly trick on him.' This went on until
his father was satisfied that he could endure anything on a golf course and not
crack.

While Earl handled the golf course and the playing schedule when his job
allowed, as well as juggling the family's financial resources to help maintain Tiger's
playing needs, his wife provided strength and stability at home. She not only
served as a taxi service to Tiger's midweek golf matches, but more importantly,
she also saw to it that he responded to all the demands of family life. She insisted
that he conduct himself properly, and particularly that he adhere to the
gentlemanly protocols of golf. At the same time, she taught him some of her own
toughness, driving home the point that when he was ahead in a match he should
not let up, but instead, try as hard as he could to overwhelm an opponent. Then,
when the match was won, he was to be a sportsman.

The 'tough love' that Earl used to shape his son's character was nothing more
than solid parenting. For example, in his very early years, Tiger was given a set of
shortened clubs and when he looked in the bag and didn't see a 1-iron, the
hardest club to hit, he asked to have one. He was told he was still too young to
generate enough clubhead speed to use it effectively; but a while later, he was out
on the driving range, using his father's 1-iron – which was almost as long as he
was tall – so effectively that there was little doubt he could handle it. His dad
promptly went out and bought him one.

In 1997, Tiger Woods took part in the U.S. Masters golf tournament. He
became the youngest ever to win the title as well as the first to win the first
major he ever played in as a professional. His twelve-stroke victory margin was
the largest ever at the Masters, and the largest in any major championship this
century.

When he sank his final putt to make par on the 18th, he spun around and
churned his arm up and down, his patented punctuation mark to signify that he
had achieved something special. A few moments later, he was in the embrace
of his parents, dissolving into tears as he hugged his father for nearly a half
minute. 'I think more than anything I was relieved it was over,' Tiger said later. 'I
think every time I hug my mom or pop after a tournament, it's over. I
accomplished my goal. And to share it with them is something special.'

When he talked by phone with President Bill Clinton a few moments later,
the First Golfer told him: 'The best shot I saw all week was the shot of you
hugging your dad.'

Conclusion of a short story by Doris Lessing

Jerry, a young English boy in South Africa, and a very good swimmer, longed to be accepted by a group of native boys. These boys were such good swimmers that they could dive to the sea bed and swim through a long tunnel, underneath a wide barrier rock, before surfacing the other side. Jerry wanted to show that he was as good as they were, by swimming through the tunnel.

But even after he had made the decision, or thought he had, he found himself sitting up on the rock and looking down into the water, and he knew that now, at this moment, when his nose had only just stopped bleeding, when his head was still sore and throbbing – this was the moment when he would try. If he did not do it now, he never

5 would. He was trembling with fear that he would not go, and he was trembling with horror at that long, long tunnel under the rock, under the sea. Even in the open sunlight the barrier rock seemed very wide and very heavy; tons of rock pressed down on where he would go. If he died there he would lie until one day – perhaps not before next year – those big boys would swim into it and find it blocked.

10 He put on his goggles, fitted them tight, tested the vacuum. His hands were shaking. Then he chose the biggest stone he could carry and slipped over the edge of the rock until half of him was in the cool, enclosing water and half in the hot sun. He looked up once at the empty sky, filled his lungs once, twice, and then sank fast to the bottom with the stone. He let it go and began to count. He took the edges of the hole in his hands and

15 drew himself into it, wriggling his shoulders in sideways as he remembered he must, kicking himself along with his feet.

Soon he was clear inside. He was in a small rock-bound hole filled with yellowish-grey water. The water was pushing him up against the roof. The roof was sharp and pained his back. He pulled himself along with his hands – fast, fast – and used his legs

20 as levers. His head knocked against something; a sharp pain dizzied him. Fifty, fifty-one, fifty-two…. He was without light, and the water seemed to press upon him with the weight of rock. Seventy-one, seventy-two…. There was no strain on his lungs. He felt like an inflated balloon, his lungs were so light and easy, but his head was pulsing.

He was being continually pressed against the sharp roof, which felt slimy as well as

25 sharp. Again he thought of octopuses, and wondered if the tunnel might be filled with weed that could tangle him. He gave himself a panicky, convulsive kick forward, ducked his head, and swam. His feet and hands moved freely, as if in open water. The hole must have widened out. He thought he must be swimming fast, and he was frightened of banging his head if the tunnel narrowed.

30 A hundred, a hundred and one…. The water paled. Victory filled him. His lungs were beginning to hurt. A few more strokes and he would be out. He was counting wildly; he said a hundred and fifteen, and then, a long time later, a hundred and fifteen again. The water was a clear jewel-green all around him. Then he saw, above his head, a crack running up through the rock. Sunlight was falling through it, showing the clean dark rock

35 of the tunnel, a single mussel shell, and darkness ahead.

He was at the end of what he could do. He looked up at the crack as if it were filled with air and not water, as if he could put his mouth to it to draw in air. A hundred and fifteen, he heard himself say inside his head – but he had said that long ago. He must go on into the blackness ahead, or he would drown. His head was swelling, his lungs cracking. A hundred and fifteen, a hundred and fifteen pounded through his head, and he feebly clutched at rocks in the dark, pulling himself forward, leaving the brief space of sunlit water behind. He felt he was dying. He was no longer quite conscious. He struggled on in the darkness between lapses into unconsciousness. An immense, swelling pain filled his head, and then the darkness cracked with an explosion of green light. His hands, groping forward, met nothing, and his feet, kicking back, propelled him out into the open sea.

He drifted to the surface, his face turned up to the air. He was gasping like a fish. He felt he would sink now and drown; he could not swim the few feet back to the rock. Then he was clutching it and pulling himself up on to it. He lay face down, gasping. He could see nothing but red-veined, clotted dark. His eyes must have burst, he thought; they were full of blood. He tore off his goggles and a gout of blood went into the sea. His nose was bleeding, and the blood had filled the goggles.

He scooped up handfuls of water from the cool, salty sea, to splash on his face, and did not know whether it was blood or salt water he tasted. After a time, his heart quieted, his eyes cleared, and he sat up. He could see the local boys, diving and playing half a mile away. He did not want them. He wanted nothing but to get back home and lie down.

In a short while, Jerry swam to shore and climbed slowly up the path to the villa. He flung himself on his bed and slept, waking at the sound of feet on the path outside. His mother was coming back. He rushed to the bathroom, thinking she must not see his face with bloodstains, or tearstains, on it. He came out of the bathroom and met her as she walked into the villa, smiling, her eyes lighting up.

'Have a nice morning?' she asked, laying her hand on his warm brown shoulder a moment.

'Oh, yes, thank you,' he said.

'You look a bit pale.' And then, sharp and anxious, 'How did you bang your head?'

'Oh, just banged it,' he told her.

She looked at him closely. He was strained. His eyes were glazed-looking. She was worried. And then she said to herself: 'Oh, don't fuss! Nothing can happen. He can swim like a fish.'

They sat down to lunch together.

'Mummy,' he said, 'I can stay under water for two minutes – three minutes, at least.' It came bursting out of him.

'Can you, darling?' she said. 'Well, I shouldn't overdo it. I don't think you ought to swim any more today.'

She was ready for a battle of wills, but he gave in at once. It was no longer of the least importance to go to the bay.

'Getting Energy from Food', an extract from a science textbook

Does food really contain energy?

We need energy to move, grow, mend our tissues when they are damaged, and just to keep ourselves alive. We get energy from our food. The energy contained in food used to be expressed in kilocalories, but this term has been replaced by kilojoules (kj). 4.2 kj of energy are required to raise the temperature of 1 kg of water through 1°C.

The amount of energy in a particular food depends on the substances which it contains. The three main kinds of food are carbohydrate, fat and protein. If we estimate the amount of energy in each of these, we can compare their energy values. Here they are:

Carbohydrate	1 gram contains 17 kj
Fat	1 gram contains 39 kj
Protein	1 gram contains 18 kj

Table 1 tells us how much energy there is in some everyday foods.

Table 1

	Kj per gram		Kj per gram
Margarine	32.2	White bread	10.6
Butter	31.2	Chips	9.9
Peanuts	24.5	Roast chicken	7.7
Milk chocolate	24.2	Eggs	6.6
Cake	18.8	Boiled potatoes	3.3
White sugar	16.5	Milk	2.7
Pork sausages	15.5	Bottled beer	1.2
Cornflakes	15.3	Boiled cabbage	0.34
Rice	15.0		

Thus, margarine and butter contain a lot of energy because they consist almost entirely of fat. At the other extreme, cabbage contains very little energy because it consists of a high percentage of water.

How much energy do we need each day?

Imagine someone lying in bed doing nothing. Even in such an inactive state, energy is needed to breathe, make the heart beat, and drive all those countless chemical reactions which keep us alive. The rate at which these 'ticking over' processes take place is called the 'basal metabolic rate'.

How much energy is needed to maintain the basal metabolic rate? It is difficult to say, because it varies from one individual to another. Very roughly, the amount needed is 7,000 kj per day. This is about the same amount of energy that would be needed to boil enough water for 100 cups of tea. This figure applies to a person who is completely at rest. It doesn't even include the energy she needs to feed herself. Scientists have tried to work out how much energy an average person needs to get through the day with the minimum effort, i.e. to get up in the morning, eat and drink and do other essential tasks, but no more. The figure is about 9,200 kj per day. A person could get enough energy to satisfy this need by eating one large white loaf a day, though, of course, this would not be a balanced diet.

Few of us spend our days like that – most of us do something. Table 2 tells us roughly how much energy is needed each day by different people.

Table 2

	Kj per day
Child 1 year old	3,000
Child 5–7 years old	7,500
Girl 12–15 years old	9,500
Boy 12–15 years old	12,000
Office worker	11,000
Factory worker	12,500
Heavy manual worker	15,000
Pregnant woman	10,000

The amount depends upon the person's age, sex and occupation. A person who spends most of the time sitting down needs far less energy than a very active person.

What happens when we eat too much?

Suppose a person eats more food than is needed for producing enough energy. What happens to the food left over? Most of it is turned into fat and stored beneath the skin. The result is that body weight increases, and he or she runs the risk of becoming fat (or obese). Obesity is caused by a person's energy input being greater than the energy output.

The most 'fattening' foods are those which provide the most energy, such as bread and margarine, cake and sweets.

How can a person lose weight? The only way is by making his or her energy input less than the output. This can be done in two different ways:

1   By taking more exercise: this will increase the energy output.
2   By eating less energy-containing food: this will decrease the energy input.

75   The first method is not very effective. A person has to take a lot of exercise to make much difference to his or her weight. For example, a man trying to lose weight may play a game of tennis for half an hour. In doing so, he loses about 700 kj of energy. After the game, he feels thirsty and has a glass of beer. The result is that he puts back all the energy he has just lost.

80   The second method is very effective if carried out properly. A person on a well-planned, weight-reducing diet can lose about 1 kg per week. Such diets contain relatively little high-energy food and a lot of low-energy food.

The best results can be obtained by combining both methods, i.e. by going on a weight-reducing diet and taking more exercise.

English Test

Reading Paper Energy for life answer booklet

First Name

Last Name

School

Write your answers in the spaces.

- The paper is 1 hour 15 minutes long.

- You have 15 minutes to read the Reading passages before answering the questions. During this time do not begin to write.

- You then have 1 hour to write your answers.

- There are 13 questions totalling 32 marks on this paper.

Answer the following questions.

Questions 1–4 are about Tiger Woods. (pages 2–3)

1 Underline the words from the following list which describe qualities that Tiger's parents taught him:

Concentration; selfishness; determination; craftiness; stability; recklessness; responsibility.

(1 mark)

2 Here is a list of events in Tiger's early life. Number them in the order in which they occur. The first one has been done for you.

1 Elrick Woods was born in Long Beach, California, in 1975.

His father tacked messages to Tiger's desk in his room.

He took up a putter and gave a perfect display of putting a golf ball.

He won a pitch, putt and drive competition against much older golfers.

He watched his father putt ball after ball into a cup.

He was out on the driving-range, using his father's 1-iron.

He asked for a 1-iron.

(1 mark)

3 What caused Tiger's father to be determined that his son would play golf well?

(3 marks)

4 The paragraph in which Tiger's father's tricks are described is linked with the one explaining his mother's role.
Write down the link sentence. Explain his mother's part in Tiger's upbringing.

(5 marks)

Questions 5–9 are about Jerry and his swimming.
(pages 4–5)

5 Before Jerry sank to the bottom of the sea, he felt a number of emotions. Underline two of the following feelings that he had:

    fear; jealousy; spite; horror; joy.

(1 mark)

6 Pick out and write down the short sentence in the second paragraph which most strongly describes the state of Jerry's nerves.

-- (1 mark)

7 Why did Jerry carry a stone with him as he got into the water?

-- (2 marks)

8 In the fifth paragraph, there is the short sentence, 'Victory filled him' (line 30). Here, the writer is using a metaphor: that is, the boy cannot literally be filled with 'victory' because it is just an idea, but the writer is expressing it that way, to strengthen the idea. Find two more phrases in the same paragraph where the writer does this.

-- (2 marks)

9 There was a great tension and excitement in the writing as Jerry struggled to swim through the tunnel and out into the open sea before he could breathe again. In the paragraph beginning, 'He drifted to the surface' (line 47), describe Jerry's feelings in your own words.
What does the reader feel at this point?

-- (4 marks)

Questions 10-13 are about the passage 'Getting energy from food.' (pages 6-8)

10 Words are often joined by a hyphen (we call them 'compounds') so that an idea can be expressed in a shorter, more effective way. These two compounds occur near the end of the passage. For each one, rewrite the same idea in your own words:

'well-planned';   'weight-reducing'.

--- (2 marks)

11 Explain why a prisoner who is not allowed out of his cell does not necessarily put on weight.

--- (2 marks)

12 The author uses questions sparingly, but they occur three times at the beginning of paragraphs, at important points in the argument. Each time, there is no need to use a question. Why do you think the author does so?

--- (3 marks)

13 Do you think it is the author's purpose to persuade people to eat more low-energy food, and so reduce weight?

--- (5 marks)

Below you will find possible answers to the Reading Test questions, with the marks awarded for those answers. Compare your answers with those that are given to see how close you came to them and whether you would have achieved the same mark.

1 The words that should be underlined are:

Concentration; determination; stability; responsibility.

Total marks: 1 (All 4 correct)

Examiner's comment

This question allows you to show an understanding of the writer's use of language at word level, and to show an understanding of the passage by interpreting information at text level.

2 The correct order is:

1 **Elrick Woods was born in Long Beach, California, in 1975.**

5 **His father tacked messages to Tiger's desk in his room.**

3 **He took up a putter and gave a perfect display of putting a golf ball.**

4 **He won a pitch, putt and drive competition against much older golfers.**

2 **He watched his father putt ball after ball into a cup.**

7 **He was out on the driving range, using his father's 1-iron.**

6 **He asked for a 1-iron.**

Total marks: 1 (This order must be totally correct)

Examiner's comment

This question enables you to show understanding of the whole passage by selecting information from different parts of it.

3   **'Because he liked the game and he had big plans for his son.'**

There are 3 marks for this question, and this answer scores none because, although what it says is true, this is not the main or most important reason for Earl's wanting Tiger to play well. This answer also uses words from the passage, instead of the pupil using his own words. Therefore, there are no marks for this answer.

'Because Earl was keen on the game but he had long been denied access to the country-club world of golf because he was black.'

This scores 1 mark because although the important point about why Earl wanted Tiger to play well is understood, it is not clearly stated, and indeed does not mention Tiger at all. In addition, some of it is just copied from the passage, and so the marker does not really know whether the pupil understands the point. Although there are no marks specifically for the style, this answer is poorly expressed, as it is not written correctly in a sentence. Therefore, 1 mark.

'Earl Woods wanted his son to play golf well, because, as a black man, he had been kept out of the well-to-do world of golf clubs.'

This scores 2 marks because, although it is now correctly written in the pupil's own words, it does not mention that Earl himself played well, and it does not say what it was that he wanted his son to do. Therefore, 2 out of 3 marks.

'Because he was a black man, Earl Woods had been excluded from the comfortable, luxurious world of golf clubs, in spite of the fact that he played well. This is what made him determined that his son would play well enough to enter the golf-club world which had been denied him.'

This scores 3 out of 3. It is well expressed in correct sentences and mentions all the relevant aspects of the situation, including Earl Woods' motivation.

Total marks: 3

Examiner's overall comment

This question enables you to comment on the writer's purpose and viewpoint, as well as showing an understanding of the passage at sentence and text levels.

4   The link sentence is: '**While Earl handled the golf course and the playing schedule when his job allowed, as well as juggling the family's financial resources to help maintain Tiger's playing needs, his wife provided strength and stability at home.**'

There is 1 mark for the whole sentence. The whole sentence is the full answer because it balances the roles of both parents and is therefore the link.

'**Tiger's mother was a taxi service to get him to his matches. She made him behave himself at matches and taught him some of her own toughness.**'

This would score 1 out of 4 marks for this question. Three of the four roles his mother played are mentioned, but most of the phrases are copied from the text.

'**Tiger's mother ran him everywhere he needed to go to golf matches, and made him take part in family life. She insisted on good conduct, and taught him how to be tough when he was ahead in a match.**'

This scores 2 out of 4 marks. All the four roles that his mother fulfilled are covered, though in a superficial way, which probably shows only a surface understanding of the text.

'**Tiger's mother had to provide transport to and from his golf matches, and also made him play his full role in family life. She was also keen on him behaving properly and like a gentleman on the golf course. However, she did not forget to teach him to have a tough attitude towards his opponent at golf.**'

This scores 3 out of 4 marks. Each role played by his mother is described in the pupil's own words and the idea that his behaviour should be appropriate to different situations is introduced.

'**Tiger's mother was obviously a strong and well-balanced person, for not only did she work hard for Tiger in the sense of providing transport for his golf matches, but she also dominated him by insisting that he played a full role in family life, for which he would have to work hard himself. Under her watchful eye, on the golf course he would have to behave properly like a gentleman. However, because of her toughness, she taught him to remain highly competitive towards his opponents until the match was over, when he should resume being a gentleman.**'

This answer scores 4 marks out of 4. Each different aspect of her influence on Tiger is set in the context of her personality, and shows a thorough understanding of the passage as a whole.

The total mark for this question is therefore 1 + 4 = 5.

Examiner's overall comment

This question enables you to show an understanding of the writer's purpose and viewpoint, to interpret information, and to comment on the structure and organisation of the text.

5   **Fear. Horror.**   Total mark: 1 (Both must be correct)

Examiner's comment

This question allows you to show an understanding of the writer's use of language at word level.

---

6   **'His hands were shaking'** (1 mark)

The full sentence is required.   Total mark: 1

Examiner's comment

This question allows you to show an understanding of the writer's use of language at sentence level.

---

7   **So that he could sink** (1 mark) **more quickly** (1 mark) *or* **fast** (1 mark).   Total marks: 2

Examiner's comment

This question allows you to show an understanding of the writer's use of language at sentence level.

---

8   **'Sunlight was falling'** (1 mark)   **'a crack running up'** (1 mark)   Total marks: 2

Examiner's comment

This question allows you to show an understanding of the writer's use of language at metaphorical and sentence levels.

---

9   *Marks are awarded only for the* **feelings** *identified.*
It does not matter what else is said about Jerry or about the reader, and it does not matter how well the answer is expressed. It is only the descriptions of Jerry's and the reader's feelings that matter.

For Jerry: **weakness; tiredness; exhaustion; relief; happiness; a sense of achievement; fear ('His eyes must have burst'); desperation ('He tore off his goggles').** Any one of these scores 1/2 mark to a maximum of 2.
For the reader: **relief; suspense; anxiety; continuing excitement; happiness; continuing tension; apprehension; uncertainty.** Any one of these scores 1/2 mark to a maximum of 2.

No one will think of all the words for the feelings, and other words may be thought of and credited with a mark if the examiner thinks they are acceptable. That is why there is a maximum of 2 for each person.

Total marks: 4
(round up to whole marks)

Examiner's comment

Here, you can show an understanding of the writer's use of language at text level and an ability to empathise with the leading character.

10 1 mark for an answer which shows an adequate understanding of the compound; 1 mark for a thorough understanding; none for a misunderstanding.

Examples:

Well-planned: **'a plan is needed'** (0 marks)
                'good planning' or **'planned efficiently and in detail'** (1 mark)

Weight-reducing: **'putting on weight'** (0 marks)
                'taking off weight' or **'weight is deliberately lost in this way'** (1 mark)

Total marks: 2

Examiner's comment

This question enables you to show an understanding of the author's use of language at word level.

---

11 *The basic idea will be that a prisoner will have a low energy output, but will not put on weight if he eats low-energy food. Marks will be awarded according to how thoroughly this is understood and the detail in which it is expressed.*

'A prisoner who does not leave his cell will not put on weight if he eats low-energy food.'

1 mark here because both sides of the problem are understood, though the first is only implied, and there is little detail in the answer.

'A prisoner who is allowed no exercise will not put on weight if he eats low-energy food such as milk, eggs and vegetables.'

2 marks here because of a thorough understanding of the question and its answer, using material from the passage, with sufficient detail.

Total marks: 2

Examiner's overall comment

This question allows you to show an understanding of the writer's purpose and viewpoint so well that you can apply it to another situation.

---

12 *This question is awarded marks according to how well the pupil has understood the use of questions to mark the stages at which the author moves on to the next problem concerning the energy-producing capacity of food.*

Examples:

'The questions make you think about food energy' (1 mark);
'The questions focus the person's mind on the problems of energy-producing food' (2 marks);
'The questions concentrate the reader on the next stage of thinking about energy-producing food' (3 marks);

Total marks: 3

Examiner's overall comment

This question enables you to identify the author's purpose by commenting on the structure and organisation of the whole text.

13   *1 mark is awarded for the expression of an opinion, whatever it is.*

Either: **Yes, it is the author's purpose to persuade people to eat low-energy food.**
Or: **No, it is not his purpose to persuade people to eat low-energy food.**
Or: **The passage is purely factual, presented in an impartial, neutral way.**

Most marks are awarded for the evidence given in support of the opinion.
Not many marks would be given for big slices of the passage just copied down.
The way the facts are used determines the quality of the answer.

'The author persuades you to eat less, because if you don't use up the food, you get fat.'

This scores one mark because the idea is crude and basic, but correct.

'The author persuades you to eat less energy by saying what energy common foods have and then how much a person uses, so if you eat more than you use, you get fat.'

This scores two marks because the general idea is understood, but it is short and poorly organised.

'It is his purpose to persuade people to eat more low-energy food because he gives a lot of information about how much energy is contained in some common foods and then some figures to show the energy used by different kinds of people. Then he tells us that what happens when we eat too much is that the extra food turns into fat, and so we should eat less energy-producing food.'

This scores three marks. It is a better balanced answer, and includes the whole argument, but there is no detail, and it is not well organised.

'I think the author's purpose is not to persuade people in any way, but to present the facts about the energy produced by food and about how much energy is needed for an average day by people, according to age, sex and occupation. He does say how excess energy causes obesity, and how fat can be reduced by diet or exercise, but the facts are just presented, and he does not say obesity is bad, or try to persuade the reader to eat low-energy foods.'

This scores four marks. All parts of the argument are sensibly presented, with some amount of detail.

Total marks: 1 + 4 = 5

Examiner's overall comment

This question enables you to identify the writer's purpose by selecting evidence for it from different parts of the passage.

Overall total: 32 marks

Where to find more help

If you have not scored full marks on all these questions, then you will find lots of guidance on how to tackle Reading Test questions in *Collins Total Revision KS3 English*.

English Test

Writing Paper

First Name _____

Last Name _____

School _____

■ Write your work on lined paper.

■ The paper is 1 hour 15 minutes long, including 15 minutes' planning time for the first task, the longer one.

■ There are two tasks.

■ The first task, the longer one, should take 45 minutes. This task has 30 marks.

■ The second task, the shorter one, should take 30 minutes. This task has 20 marks.

■ Plan your answer for the first task on the planning page opposite the task. This page will not be marked.

■ Write your answers in the Writing Paper answer booklet.

LONGER TASK

Game On!

Write the story of any physical activity in which you have taken part.

This could be anything, from a football, hockey, cricket or netball match, to skating or swimming, or a ride in a fairground or theme park, or just going for a walk.

Whatever you write about, include:

- thoughts and feelings you have before the event;
- a description of what you did;
- your feelings of satisfaction or pleasure which were produced by the activity.

(30 marks)

Use this page to plan your work. (This page will not be marked.)

Thoughts and feelings before event

-
-
-
-
-

What you did

What happened

Any problems or difficulties

How it ended

Feelings

-
-
-
-
-

Reasons for feelings

-
-
-
-
-

SHORTER TASK

A Walking Holiday

Imagine that you have a cousin who lives in a distant town. His or her Youth Club leader has written to invite you to join a walking holiday with the club for a week in August.

Write a letter to the leader, accepting his offer.

In thanking him for the invitation, refer to your cousin, who may be a boy or a girl, saying what great friends you have been for many years.

Tell him:

- what experience you have had of walking holidays
- what you hope this holiday will be like
- how you hope to enjoy it.

There is no need to set out the letter in any formal way.
Address the Youth leader as 'Dear Mr Lee'.

(20 marks)

Longer Task and Shorter Task

Pages 23–30 aim to help you mark, and improve, the answer you have given to the Longer writing task on page 20. Pages 31–36 aim to help you mark, and improve, the answer you have given to the Shorter writing task on page 22.

In order to work out what mark you would be awarded for each answer, do the following:

1 Read the 'Guidance on Key Features' given for each mark range.

2 Read carefully the sample answer linked to each mark range. By reading all these extracts, you will see the improvement in the writing from one mark range to the next.

3 Of course, the content of your writing will not be the same as the content in the extracts, but you should be able to tell if the quality of your writing is similar.

4 Now see if you can match *your* answer to a mark range. If you are unsure, ask someone you can trust – your teacher, a relative or a friend – to help you.

5 Then award yourself a mark within the mark range. Choose a low mark if you feel your writing only just fits in the range and a high mark if you feel it is at the top of the range.

6 Once you have decided what mark your answer would probably be given, look at the guidance given under 'How to improve your answer'. This suggests what you need to do to improve your answer so that you can do better next time, and achieve a higher mark. If you like, re-write your answer and then see if it fits the features described for the mark range above.

WRITING PAPER – LONGER TASK
Guidance and sample answers

How well did you do?   *3-9 marks*

Guidance on key features

If your answer deserves a mark in this mark range:

- You will have used full stops and capital letters correctly, showing that you can write in properly constructed sentences. You will also have used adjectives and connectives such as 'because', 'when', 'if' and 'although'. You will have used different tenses and even adverbial phrases (e.g. 'by concentrating hard…').

- You will have written a title and will have used paragraphs which begin with a topic sentence (e.g. 'I got excited about…') and which include some details of what you did.

- You will have begun the story by saying clearly what you are writing about. You will have written in the first person (e.g. 'I walked to the rollercoaster…') and will have described the event in some detail, mentioning some feelings you had, and especially some thoughts which finish off your story well.

Extract from a sample answer in this mark range

Gosthorpe Theme Park

In the summer holidays, we went to Gosthorpe theme park. It was the best day of the holidays so I want to write about it.

It is about twenty miles away and Mum and Dad decided we would go there because we did not go away on holiday this year, but just on day trips. There was a rollercoaster ride they said was the biggest in the country. Dad said my young brother, Jack, who is only six, was too young to go on it, but I could go.

I was excited about going on it, but a bit afraid too, because if I fell off I might have got hurt or even killed. When we got there, I went on it because I did not want to look scared by not going on. My dad paid and when I was on it, I was frightened, as it climbed slowly up a big rise, then I shut my eyes and held tight on to the metal bar in front of me when it looped round and we went upside down.

When I got off, my legs felt a bit funny but it was good being on the ground. I felt really proud that I had done it. My mum smiled at me and Jack looked up and asked what it was like.

"Okay." I said. "You will have to have a go when you are bigger."

24

How to improve your answer

1 Try to develop more of a sense of your own character by giving more detailed thoughts and feelings. Occasionally, use a simile or metaphor.

2 Use connectives to link ideas and events within the same sentence or between different sentences.

3 Try to use clauses to give more ideas (e.g. 'The ride was so exciting that I wanted it to continue…').

4 Try to vary the tenses, using adverbial phrases (e.g. 'By being determined…') or by the use of modals (e.g. 'I would have enjoyed it more, if I could have gone on it again.').

5 Make each paragraph lead on to the next logically by using adverbial connectives such as 'Luckily I hadn't eaten before I got on the ride...' Vary the lengths of paragraphs and sentences.

6 Use a good range of punctuation marks, including those needed for direct speech.

7 Use impersonal forms to increase variety (e.g. 'It was a testing time for me…')

How well did you do?   *10–16 marks*

Guidance on key features

If your answer deserves a mark in this mark range:

- You will have kept the reader's interest by such techniques as:
  – using direct speech
  – including details of your thoughts and feelings
  – including figurative language, e.g. similes or metaphors, to give some force to your feelings.

- Your paragraphs and sentences will be varied in length because you will have used connectives such as 'however' and connecting clauses such as 'When I felt this…'.

- You will have varied the verb tenses by using modals such as 'I would have been less scared if I could have got straight on…'.

- You will have used a good range of punctuation and will have introduced impersonal forms to add further variety to your expression (e.g. 'This was quite a challenge…').

Extract from a sample answer in this mark range

A visit to Gosthorpe Theme Park

I was extremely disappointed that we were not going away on holiday this year. However, I felt much better when our parents told me and Jack, my younger brother, that we were going on a trip to Gosthorpe Theme Park.

I had heard my friends at school talking about the new rollercoaster ride, the biggest in the country, and I wanted to tell them that I had been on it too.

When we got there, we went to the rollercoaster first. My stomach felt like a cage full of butterflies as I queued to get on. I would have been less scared if I could have climbed straight on without queuing. However, when my turn came, I got into the car quickly by being determined to do it. This was quite a test for me, because I used to be shy and weak, but this challenge had to be met.

As I sat down, I could not stop looking at the solid metal bar in front of me, and I grabbed it tightly. As we went slowly up the steep climb, I looked at the bar and took deep breaths. Then we went over the loop, and when we were upside down, I closed my eyes and put my head between my knees. I know that some people looked about and waved their arms, but they had probably been on the ride before.

Soon it was over and I got off.

"Well done," said Mum. "Jack and I saw you put your head down."

"Yes. Well, it's scary going upside down," I said, "but I will be fine next time, and perhaps Jack can come."

How to improve your answer

1 Keep a consistent narrative voice, tracing your thoughts and feelings, so that you can lead the reader through the story, controlling what he or she feels. Mix information with thoughts and comments.

2 Carefully organise the beginning and ending, to create interest at first and to produce satisfaction at the end.

3 Vary the length and structure of your sentences by using subordinate clauses and phrases to develop plot/thoughts/feelings. Sometimes, make the style more formal by using passive constructions (e.g. 'Customers were told to form a queue...').

4 Use a range of verb tenses, including modals, occasionally adding adverbial and noun phrases.

5 Develop links between paragraphs, and use a wide range of punctuation to give clarity to your narrative.

6 At the end of the story, try to bring together the different threads you have mentioned during the course of it. The story must have a deliberately organised shape and a number of strands in it to manipulate the reader.

How well did you do?

17–23 marks

Guidance on key features

If your answer deserves a mark in this mark range:

- You will have carefully shaped and controlled your story so that at different points you mention different threads. Having arrested the reader's attention at the beginning, and having regulated it throughout the narrative, you will have brought those threads together in a satisfying way at the conclusion.

- You will have kept a consistent narrative voice, mixing information with thoughts and feelings.

- You will have varied the length of your sentences by using subordinate clauses and phrases.

- You will have used a wide variety of verb forms and tenses, including modals in compound and complex sentences.

- You may have made the tone of your writing more formal in places by using passive constructions.

Extract from a sample answer in this mark range

A visit to Gosthorpe Theme Park

I hated my dad. He said that he could not take time off for our family to go away during the summer holidays and that we would have to make do with occasional trips. I was really depressed. What a miserable summer it would be.

It was not as bad for the others. Jack, my brother, was only six, and he hardly knew the difference between school and holidays because they often went on excursions at his school. Because my mum didn't have a job outside our home, her life seemed to me like one long holiday, although she said it wasn't. I was at secondary school, where we had to work so hard that I really needed a holiday.

Then, one day, Dad said that we could all go on a trip to Gosthorpe Theme Park. I was really excited. My friends at school had been talking about it for months. A few weeks earlier, the biggest rollercoaster in the country had been opened there. I was apprehensive about going on it, but, at the same time, I was determined to show the family and everyone else that I was not frightened to take a ride.

As we arrived at the park, we could see the rollercoaster dominating the scene, looming menacingly over the whole park, a sinister monster that was daring people to take a ride. Everyone who had paid was directed to a queueing area and my stomach was churning like a concrete mixer.

Suddenly, I found myself in the car, sitting on the hard seat, holding the front bar very tightly, and making steady progress up the steep incline before the loop. As I looked down, I hoped to see my family: I would have waved to them had I been able to spot them, but I couldn't. From the top, we plunged down into space, and a huge force, like a giant hand, forced us up again and over the loop upside down. Doggedly, I hung on as we careered up and down the rails and round bends that tried to fling me out sideways.

I walked on jellied legs to rejoin my family.

"Okay then?" asked Mum.

"Sure," I said with a confidence which belied my true feelings. "This is better than lying on a beach in some exotic place. I can't wait to go again and take Jack with me."

Now, I told myself, I had something to tell my friends.

How to improve your answer

1   Choose a deliberate style to sustain the narrative voice by which you are relating your thoughts and feelings about the event.

2   Continue to vary the sentence patterns by including a variety of subordinate clauses and phrases. Use a mixture of short, simple sentences, and compound ones.

3   Consciously structure the whole story by alternating between dialogue and narration, reflection and plot. Try to be succinct and imaginative.

4   Use a wide range of punctuation to give clarity and create specific effects, e.g. colons, dashes, semi-colons, ellipsis.

5   Keep the narrative viewpoint consistent, strong, effective and convincing.

6   Make sure the whole story is crafted, shaped and controlled for the interest and entertainment of the reader.

How well did you do?　　　　　*24–30 marks*

Guidance on key features

If your answer deserves a mark in this mark range:

- You will have maintained a consistent narrative voice, mixing information, an account of events and interpretations of your thoughts and feelings.

- Your punctuation will be very varied with a high degree of accuracy.

- You will have varied the sentence patterns with appropriate subordinate clauses and phrases. You will have used simple, complex and compound sentences to achieve specific effects.

- You will have alternated dialogue with plot, reflection with description. You will have imbued your narrative with an inspiring imaginative quality. Indeed, the whole story will have been controlled and manipulated with the purpose of giving the reader the best possible literary experience.

Extract from a sample answer in this mark range

A moment of triumph in Gosthorpe Adventure Park

I was in despair. I hated my dad. He had just told our family – Mum, my six-year-old brother Jack, and me – that he couldn't take enough time off work this year for us all to go away for a summer holiday. What a miserable prospect – the long, glorious summer holidays, and we were not going away.

Mum didn't work, and Jack seemed to play all the time at his Infants' school: it was me who needed a holiday. We were pushed so hard at our highly-competitive secondary school that I felt I really needed a holiday – "rest and recuperation", as our beloved form teacher put it!

Suddenly, the gloom lifted and the clouds of misery were dispelled. Dad had said that we could go for a day out at Gosthorpe Adventure Park, a theme park which had separated recently from its associated wildlife park and had considerably expanded. Among its recently acquired attractions was a new rollercoaster – the biggest in the country, it was claimed.

I had envied my friends at school, who had visited the park on the day the new rollercoaster was opened. It was, by their accounts, a terrifying ride – white knuckles, and hearts in mouths.

It did indeed seem intimidating as we approached it. It towered over all the smaller attractions, at once inviting and defiant. It sent out a challenge to everyone.

I felt the challenge very keenly. I had been shy, withdrawn and timid when I was younger, but now I longed to prove my adventurous spirit. Everyone was directed by stewards towards a narrow entrance gate. I would not have felt so nervous if I had not had to queue. My fear was in my mouth. My tongue was dry. I hoped I would have the courage to get in and hold on.

Then I was in the car, which was climbing remorselessly towards the loop. I looked down for my family, but could not see them. The sudden downward plunge took my breath away. An immensely powerful pressure forced us up again and we travelled the top of the loop upside down. Head down, eyes closed, I gripped the bar. We were careering along again, whirling round corners, and then screeching to a halt.

My dad was putting his arm round my shoulders.

"Was it worth it?" he asked.

"You bet," I replied. "That was better than baking on a beach."

"Well done!" said Mum, and Jack looked up wide-eyed.

"Can I come next time?" he asked.

"Of course you can," I replied, confidently playing the elder-brother role. And I thought of my new-found credibility at school.

WRITING PAPER - SHORTER TASK
Guidance and sample answers

How well did you do?   *3-8 marks*

Guidance on key features

If your answer deserves a mark in this mark range:

- You will have given Mr Lee a written acceptance of his invitation to join the holiday.

- You will have thanked him and referred to your cousin, mentioning that your friendship with him or her makes you sure that you will enjoy yourselves. As you will have written in the first person, your tone will be friendly. You will have been quite emphatic about your gratitude to him and positive about your hopes for a good holiday.

- Most of your sentences will be simply constructed and your use of full stops will be mostly accurate. A few sentences may have been expanded by using connectives such as 'when', 'and', 'but' and 'then'.

- You will have written in paragraphs and will have used some variations in verb tenses – at least the past, present and future tenses.

- You will have kept your vocabulary simple so that you will have spelt most of the words correctly, although you need to take care with words that sound the same, e.g. there/their; were/where; practice/practise.

Extract from a sample answer in this mark range

Dear Mr Lee,

I am writing to thank you for the invitation to join your Youth Club walking holiday. My cousin, Chris, had told me about it. Then I received your letter. In it, you told me where you are going.

I think the Yorkshire Dales is a beautiful part of the country, and I went there for a day's walk a few years ago when we were on holiday in Scarborough.

I want to tell you how very grateful I am to you for inviting me, because I am such close friends with Chris. We live a long way away from each other, and this will give us a chance to be together for a whole week. I like open air things, so I am sure I will enjoy it.

How to improve your answer

1   Give more details about yourself, your interests and character, and your hopes for the holiday.

2   Make your sentences more varied in length and construction, and increase the variation and complexity of the verbs (e.g. 'If we can cover twenty miles a day, that will have made me very fit by the end of the holiday.').

3   Keep the tone friendly and personal, and the style direct.

4   Try to widen the range of your punctuation.

5   Widen the range of your vocabulary by using adjectives and adverbs.

6   Clearly link your paragraphs, and develop the ideas within your letter.

7   Concentrate on spelling simple and common words correctly, especially words which sound the same, e.g. weather/whether; affect/effect.

How well did you do?   *9–14 marks*

Guidance on key features

If your answer deserves a mark in this mark range:

- You will have given the person to whom you are writing a fairly detailed picture of your character and interests so that he knows plenty about you before the holiday.

- You will have given a sense of looking forward to the holiday. You will have presented the information in such a way as to give Mr Lee an impression of friendliness and honesty.

- You will have varied the length of your sentences and also used a variety of verb tenses.

- Your punctuation and spelling will be mainly correct, and your vocabulary reasonably wide.

- Your paragraphs will be linked by a number of opening phrases, and there will be a development of ideas throughout the whole letter.

Extract from a sample answer in this mark range

Dear Mr Lee,

It was very kind of you to invite me to join the walking holiday which you have planned for your Youth Club this year.

As you might expect, my cousin, Chris, had already given me some details in a letter, telling me how the invitation arose in the first place. Chris and I are such great friends that I am sure I will have an enjoyable time with you, and that the other members of the club will make me feel welcome. I am really looking forward to it.

As far as the activity itself is concerned, you may like to know that I have taken part in a few sponsored walks of up to thirty miles. I have also been on camping holidays with other friends, and in general I am very keen on the outdoor life. Therefore, I hope I can contribute to the spirit of adventure and happiness that I am sure is characteristic of your members.

Please let me know of any particular equipment you would like me to bring, and let's hope the weather is sunny!

How to improve your answer

1   Use more complex sentences, and continue to vary the length of those sentences by using subordinate clauses and a range of verb tenses, including modals (e.g. 'I wouldn't have been able to …').

2   Continue to develop the links between your paragraphs by using specific devices such as temporal and causal phrases. Link ideas within the paragraphs by using connecting phrases (e.g. 'When I had done that …', 'At the same time …').

3   Organise your writing to give as much information, clearly, to Mr Lee as is necessary for him to plan your inclusion in the activities and arrangements for the holiday.

4   Use punctuation clearly to make the structure of your sentences clear.

5   Continue to make your tone informal and friendly, which is appropriate to a personal letter.

6   Spell complex and regular words correctly, but be very careful with words that are commonly misspelled, e.g. receive, brief, weird.

How well did you do?

15–19 marks

Guidance on key features

If your answer deserves a mark in this mark range:

- You will have given Mr Lee enough information about your character, your interests and your likes and dislikes to enable him to include you in various arrangements and activities.

- You will also have linked your paragraphs by various devices, and connected the ideas within the paragraphs to give a sense of development to the ideas in the whole letter.

- You will have varied the length of your sentences and used a number of different verb tenses within them.

- Your punctuation and spelling will be clear and accurate.

- Bearing in mind that this is a personal letter, you will, by your informal tone, have given Mr Lee an impression of your friendly, open and honest personality.

Extract from a sample answer in this mark range

Dear Mr Lee,

It was very generous of you to invite me to participate in the walking holiday that you are arranging for your Youth Club this year.

Because my cousin, Chris, had previously explained by letter how the invitation came about, I had been anticipating your letter with some enthusiasm. I love long-distance walking, and can think of no more beautiful an area to do it in than the Yorkshire Dales. I hope we spend a lot of our time walking.

As long as Chris and I can be together, there is no possibility of my not enjoying the holiday, so close are our characters and outlooks. I have completed many sponsored walks, of distances ranging from three to thirty miles, and I have considerable experience of camping with my friends. I can be described as a team player, but at the same time, I am perfectly happy undertaking tasks on my own, if your planned activities involve this for different members. Whatever the arrangements you are making, I am sure I will play my role supportively and with relish.

Thank you once again, Mr Lee, for inviting me, and if you are able to send me details in advance of arrangements, regulations and equipment needed, I will do my best to comply with everything you require.

How to improve your answer

1   Ensure that you have given Mr Lee, and therefore the reader, sufficient information about your character, interests, tastes and experience to give a complete picture of yourself in the context of the potential holiday.

2   Continue to develop the way you vary the length and structure of your sentences, using a range of verb forms, appropriate subordinate clauses, and a variety of phrases. Both compound and complex sentences must be well under control.

3   Use as wide a vocabulary as is appropriate, but, at the same time, keep the expression succinct and economical.

4   Plan the whole letter from the outset, bearing in mind the number of paragraphs you intend to use, along with the phrases by which you link each one to its preceding one, and the way in which you will develop the ideas within each paragraph.

5   Make sure the punctuation and spelling are correct, being especially careful with irregular and complicated words.

6   Maintain and develop your deliberately informal style, and the engagingly personal and friendly tone which you have established.

How well did you do?   *20 marks*

Guidance on key features

If your answer deserves the very top mark:

- You will have given Mr Lee all the information which is relevant to the holiday. He needs to know something about your experience of such a holiday, your character and ability, and to some extent what you expect to do.

- You will also have developed the various aspects of style and organisation in letter writing to the highest quality that can reasonably be expected for someone of your age. Your sentences will be of varied length and structure, showing a range of verb forms and a variety of subordinate clauses and phrases. You will have used vocabulary which is exactly right to express all your ideas without undue elaboration.

- Your whole letter will have been well-planned, each paragraph linked to the one before. Ideas within each paragraph will be sequenced to produce a continuous development.

- Words will be correctly spelt and sentences correctly punctuated, using an informal style which communicates a friendly, personal tone.

Extract from a sample answer achieving this top mark

Dear Mr Lee,

I much appreciate your generosity in inviting me to participate in the walking holiday that you are arranging for your Youth Club this year. I am sure it will be an experience that I will value for many years to come.

As you will be aware, my cousin, Chris, had already written to me to explain how the invitation arose, and so it was with eager anticipation that I awaited your letter. I expect that Chris will also have told you that I love long-distance walking, especially in an area with all the natural attractions of the Yorkshire Dales.

The prospect of spending a holiday with Chris is one that I am greatly excited by, for we have so much in common in terms of character and outlook that it is simply not possible that I will not enjoy the holiday. Among experiences that Chris and I have shared have been family walking holidays, camping with uniformed groups, and sponsored walks.

I am sure that your members will make me welcome, as I usually relate easily and happily to people that I meet, and am able to co-operate with others within a group or undertake individual ventures if they are included in your programme.

I am so grateful for the invitation to join you, that I will be willing to adapt to any arrangement you make, and to comply with any regulations which are necessary. If it is convenient to you, perhaps you would send me details of any special equipment or clothing I might need.

I am really looking forward to meeting you and, as I said earlier, I have no doubt that I will enjoy the holiday enormously.

English Test

Shakespeare Paper

The paper is **45 minutes** long.

You may choose to write about **one** of three Shakespeare plays:

- *Macbeth*
- *Much Ado About Nothing*
- *Henry V*

This paper assesses your reading and understanding of your chosen play and has **18 marks**. It consists of **one task** on two extracts from the scenes chosen for special study in each of the plays.

Turn to **page 38** for the *Macbeth* paper.

Turn to **page 48** for the *Much Ado About Nothing* paper.

Turn to **page 57** for the *Henry V* paper.

You have 45 minutes to write your answer to the following task.

MACBETH

Act 3 Scene 1 (lines 114–end) and Act 3 Scene 2 (lines 22–46)
Act 3 Scene 4 (lines 49–98)

In these scenes, Macbeth relies on the murderers to rid him of Banquo and Fleance.

Imagine you are Macbeth. Trace your feelings during these extracts. Write in the first person (as if you are Macbeth).

(18 marks)

Reading extracts for MACBETH

In this extract, Macbeth is persuading two murderers that Banquo hates all of them and must be killed, together with Fleance, his son. Lady Macbeth tries to console her husband, but his mind is in torment.

Act 3 Scene 1 (line 114 to end)

MACBETH Both of you
Know Banquo was your enemy.

SEC. MUR. True, my lord.

MACBETH So is he mine; and in such bloody distance
That every minute of his being thrusts
Against my near'st of life: and though I could
With bare-fac'd power sweep him from my sight
And bid my will avouch it, yet I must not,
For certain friends that are both his and mine,
Whose loves I may not drop, but wail his fall
Whom I myself struck down; and thence it is
That I to your assistance do make love,
Masking the business from the common eye
For sundry weighty reasons.

SEC. MUR. We shall, my lord,
Perform what you command us.

FIRST MUR. Though our lives –

MACBETH Your spirits shine through you. Within this hour at most
I will advise you where to plant yourselves,
Acquaint you with the perfect spy o' the time,
The moment on't; for it must be done tonight,
And something from the palace; always thought
That I require a clearness: and with him –
To leave no rubs nor botches in the work –
Fleance his son, that keeps him company,
Whose absence is no less material to me
Than is his father's, must embrace the fate
Of that dark hour. Resolve yourselves apart;
I'll come to you anon.

SEC. MUR. We are resolv'd, my lord.

MACBETH I'll call upon you straight: abide within.

[Exeunt murderers]

It is concluded: Banquo, thy soul's flight,
If it find heaven, must find it out tonight.

Act 3 Scene 2 (lines 22–46)

MACBETH Duncan is in his grave;
After life's fitful fever he sleeps well;
Treason has done his worst: nor steel, nor poison,
Malice domestic, foreign levy, nothing
Can touch him further.

LADY M. Come on; gentle my lord, sleek o'er your rugged looks;
Be bright and jovial among our guests tonight.

MACBETH So shall I, love; and so, I pray, be you.
Let your remembrance apply to Banquo;
Present him with eminence, both with eye and tongue:
Unsafe the while, that we
Must lave our honours in these flattering streams,
And make our faces vizards to our hearts,
Disguising what they are.

LADY M. You must leave this.

MACBETH O! Full of scorpions is my mind, dear wife;
Thou know'st that Banquo and his Fleance lives.

LADY M. But in them nature's copy's not eterne.

MACBETH There's comfort yet; they are assailable;
Then be thou jocund. Ere the bat hath flown
His cloister'd flight, ere, to black Heacate's summons
The shard-borne beetle with his drowsy hums
Hath rung night's yawning peal, there shall be done
A deed of dreadful note.

LADY M. What's to be done?

MACBETH Be innocent of the knowledge, dearest chuck,
Till thou applaud the deed.

In this extract, Macbeth is hosting his banquet; he has just learnt that the murderers have killed Banquo but Fleance has escaped. Macbeth imagines he sees the ghost of Banquo sitting in his chair, while Lady Macbeth tries to calm him down.

Act 3 Scene 4 (lines 49–98)

MACBETH   Which of you have done this?

LORDS   What, my good lord?

MACBETH   Thou canst not say I did it: never shake
Thy gory locks at me.

ROSS   Gentlemen, rise; his highness is not well.

LADY M.   Sit, worthy friends: my lord is often thus,
And hath been from his youth: pray you, keep seat;
The fit is momentary; upon a thought
He will again be well. If much you note him
You shall offend him and extend his passion:
Feed and regard him not. Are you a man?

MACBETH   Ay, and a bold one, that dare look on that
Which might appal the devil.

LADY M.   O proper stuff!
This is the very painting of your fear;
This is the air-born dagger which, you said
Led you to Duncan. O! these flaws and starts –
Impostors to true fear – would well become
A woman's story at a winter's fire,
Authoriz'd by her grandam. Shame itself!
Why do you make such faces? When all's done
You look but on a stool.

MACBETH   Prithee, see there! Behold! Look! Lo! How say you?
Why, what care I? If thou canst nod, speak too.
If charnel-houses and our graves must send
Those that we bury back, our monuments
Shall be the maws of kites.

[Ghost disappears.]

LADY M.   What! Quite unmanned in folly?

MACBETH   If I stand here, I saw him.

LADY M.   Fie, for shame!

MACBETH   Blood hath been shed ere now, I' the olden time,
           Ere human statute purg'd the gentle weal;
           Ay, and since too, murders have been perform'd
           Too terrible for the ear: the times have been,
           That, when the brains were out, the man would die,
           And there an end; but now they rise again,
           With twenty mortal murders on their crowns,
           And push us from our stools: this is more strange
           Than such a murder is.

LADY M.   My worthy lord,
           Your noble friends do lack you.

MACBETH   I do forget.
           Do not muse at me, my most worthy friends;
           I have a strange infirmity, which is nothing
           To those that know me. Come, love and health to all;
           Then, I'll sit down. Give me some wine; fill full.
           I drink to the general joy of the whole table,
           And to our dear friend Banquo, whom we miss;
           Would he were here! To all and him, we thirst,
           And all to all.

LORDS   Our duties, and the pledge.

           [Re-enter ghost]

MACBETH   Avaunt! And quit my sight! Let the earth hide thee!
           Thy bones are marrowless, thy blood is cold;
           Thou hast no speculation in those eyes
           Which thou dost glare with.

LADY M.   Think of this, good peers,
           But as a thing of custom: 'tis no other;
           Only it spoils the pleasure of the time.

MACBETH

In order to work out what mark you would be awarded for your answer, do the following:

1   Read the **'Guidance on key features'** for each mark range.

2   Read carefully the **sample answers** for each mark range. These provide an example of the sorts of points that would be made by a student working within this mark range. Of course, you will not have written exactly the same remarks, but you should be able to tell if the **quality** of your writing is similar.

3   Now see if you can match *your* answer to a mark range. If you are unsure, ask someone you can trust – a relative, friend or teacher – to help you. Then, within the range, decide whether your answer deserves the top, middle or lowest mark. Is your answer a very good fit within the range (top mark), a reasonable fit (middle mark) or does it barely fit within it (lowest mark)?

4   Once you have decided what mark your answer would probably be given, look at **'How to improve your answer'**. This suggests what you need to do to improve your answer so that you can do better next time, and achieve a higher mark.

How well did you do?   *3–6 marks*

Guidance on key features

If your answer deserves a mark in this mark range:

- You will have written in the first person, as instructed, and you will have included material from both extracts.

- You will have mentioned relevant details of what happened and you will have made some mention of Macbeth's feelings, which is the focus of the task.

- You will have attempted to use quotations to support your points.

Extract from a sample answer in this mark range

I wanted Banquo and Fleance to be killed because since the witches' predictions of becoming king and Thane of Cawdor came true, I was worried that Banquo's prediction would come true as well.

I thought the murderers would do the job and I could be settled. I was having a banquet when they came and told me they had killed Banquo but not Fleance. I was really disappointed. Then I went mad because I saw Banquo's ghost sitting in my place at the table, "Never shake thy gory locks at me!"

My wife was very good and tried to make excuses and settle me down but I kept going on and she had to send them away in the end.

How to improve your answer

1   The focus of the task is Macbeth's feelings. Try to express these more strongly.

2   Use more quotations from the scenes to support your points.

3   Identify Macbeth's worst fear and spend more time developing that aspect.

How well did you do?   *7–10 marks*

Guidance on key features

If your answer deserves a mark in this mark range:

- You will have clearly understood Macbeth's worry and disappointment and you will attempt to focus on his feelings rather than on what happened.

- You will mention that, although Lady Macbeth was to some extent shut out of Macbeth's thoughts, he was rescued by her at the banquet.

Extract from a sample answer in this mark range

> Even though I was now king, I was not happy. Banquo knew about the witches and, even worse, the last prediction they made was for Banquo, saying that his descendants would be kings. That's why I organised some murderers to get rid of him and Fleance for me. I dared not kill them myself. It would be too risky.
>
> I persuaded the murderers that Banquo was the cause of all their troubles. It was really easy. I didn't tell my wife because she would only worry, but she knew that my mind was troubled,
>
> "How now, my lord! Why do you keep alone,
> Of sorriest fancies your companions making."
>
> When the murderers came back during the banquet and told me they had killed Banquo, I was very glad, but then they said that Fleance had escaped, which was a disaster.
>
> I couldn't keep my mind on the banquet and I saw Banquo, covered in blood, sitting in my chair. I started shouting at him that it wasn't me and my wife had to cover for me. When she saw that I had spoiled the banquet, she sent the guests away, saying I was ill.

How to improve your answer

1 Concentrate less on telling the story; include only those sections connected directly with Macbeth's feelings.

2 Use quotations which express specifically how Macbeth was feeling at various stages of the extracts.

3 Explain how the nature of Macbeth's fear changes across these extracts.

45

How well did you do? *11–14 marks*

Guidance on key features

If your answer deserves a mark in this mark range:

- You will have focused well on the task and will have considered Macbeth's feelings at different stages.

- You may not have used many direct quotations, but your understanding of, for example, the motivation of the murderers, is quite clear.

- Your final paragraph will express Macbeth's loss of control.

Extract from a sample answer in this mark range

I thought that I would be happy once I became King of Scotland, but this was not so. I was anxious about Banquo, who knew all about the witches' prophecies. Not only that, the final prophecy had told him his heirs would be kings, so he was a danger to me on two counts. So, as he knew too much I employed two murderers to kill him. I took some trouble to persuade them that he was their enemy and it was his fault they had not got on in life. I told them the time and the place, and that they must kill Fleance too, to make a clean job of it.

I thought this would end my worries but I was in some torment while I was waiting for the news of his death. I couldn't tell my dear wife, wanting her to be, "innocent of the knowledge".

Nothing could express my disappointment when the murderers told me that Fleance had escaped. I was so churned up inside that I thought I saw the dead Banquo sitting in my seat and shaking his head at me. I don't know what I said but my wife thought it was too much. She sent away our guests, saying I was ill and getting worse by the minute.

How to improve your answer

1 Having expressed Macbeth's feelings clearly, use quotations to illustrate the varying intensity of these feelings.

2 Develop the implications of the loss of Macbeth's control at the banquet.

3 Develop Lady Macbeth's role and his feelings towards her.

How well did you do?   *15–18 marks*

Guidance on key features

If your answer deserves a mark in this mark range:

- Your language will emphasise the intensity of Macbeth's emotions.

- Your quotations will be concise and well-chosen to illustrate Macbeth's despair.

- You will have conveyed the depths of Macbeth's feelings at different points of the action.

Extract from a sample answer in this mark range

I am tormented by the events of the last few days. Kingship did not bring a sense of security; the witches have already been right on two counts: I am Thane of Cawdor and king. Therefore I could not get out of my mind their prediction that Banquo's heirs would be rulers. I had no choice but to take decisive action again and hire some cutthroats to remove Banquo and his son.

It was easy to persuade the wretched villains that Banquo had been responsible for all that was miserable in their lives, that his "heavy hand hath bow'd you to the grave and beggar'd yours for ever". It was less easy dealing with my wife, as she had noticed my "sorriest fancies". I admitted, in my black mood, that I almost envied the peace that Duncan was experiencing in death, "nor steel, nor poison, Malice domestic, foreign levy, nothing can touch him further".

My worst fears were realised when the murderers reported back that they had only achieved half of their mission: Fleance escaped. I can't describe my anguish, which played tricks on my mind and made me hallucinate: I clearly saw the murdered Banquo and addressed him, "Let the earth hide thee! Thy bones are marrowless, thy blood is cold; Thou hast no speculation in those eyes." Even worse, my torment was witnessed by all my guests, who must now be suspicious.

You have 45 minutes to write your answer to the following task.

MUCH ADO ABOUT NOTHING

Act 1 Scene 1 (lines 120–204)
Act 2 Scene 3 (lines 240–266)

At the beginning of the play, the characters reveal
themselves to the audience by what they say.

**What different opinions do you think the audience forms
of Benedick during these two scenes?**

(18 marks)

Reading extracts for
MUCH ADO ABOUT NOTHING

In this extract, Benedick and Beatrice enjoy teasing one another, giving their negative views on marriage and the opposite sex. Benedick then gives Claudio the benefit of his advice.

Act 1 Scene 1 (lines 120–204)

BEATRICE   I wonder that you will still be talking, Signior Benedick; nobody marks you.

BENE.   What! My dear Lady Disdain, are you yet living?

BEAT.   Is it possible Disdain should die while she hath such meet food to feed it as Signior Benedick? Courtesy itself must convert to disdain, if you come in her presence.

BENE.   Then is courtesy a turncoat. But it is certain I am loved of all ladies, only you excepted; and I would I could find in my heart that I had not a hard heart; for, truly, I love none.

BEAT.   A dear happiness to women: they would else have been troubled with a pernicious suitor. I thank God and my cold blood, I am of your humour for that: I had rather hear my dog bark at a crow than a man swear he loves me.

BENE.   God keep your ladyship still in that mind; so some gentleman or other shall 'scape a predestinate scratched face.

BEAT.   Scratching could not make it worse, an 'twere such a face as yours were.

BENE.   Well, you are a rare parrot-teacher.

BEAT.   A bird of my tongue is better than a beast of yours.

BENE.   I would my horse had the speed of your tongue, and so good a continuer. But keep your way, i' God's name; I have done.

BEAT.   You always end with a jade's trick: I know you of old.

DON PEDRO   This is the sum of all, Leonato: Signior Claudio and Signior Benedick, my dear friend Leonato hath invited you all. I tell him we shall stay here at the least a month, and he heartily prays some occasion may detain us longer: I dare swear he is no hypocrite, but prays from his heart.

LEON. If you swear, my lord, you shall not be forsworn. *[to Don John]* Let me bid you welcome, my lord: being reconciled to the prince your brother, I owe you all duty.

D. JOHN I thank you. I am not of many words, but I thank you.

LEON. Please it your Grace lead on?

D. PEDRO Your hand, Leonato; we will go together.

[Exeunt all but Claudio and Benedick]

CLAUD. Benedick, didst thou note the daughter of Signior Leonato?

BENE. I noted her not; but I looked on her.

CLAUD. Is she not a modest young lady?

BENE. Do you question me, as an honest man should do, for my simple true judgment; or would you have me speak after my custom, as being a professed tyrant to their sex?

CLAUD. No; I pray thee speak in sober judgment.

BENE. Why, i'faith, methinks she's too low for a high praise, too brown for a fair praise, and too little for a great praise: only this commendation I can afford her, that were she other than she is, she were unhandsome, and being no other but as she is, I do not like her.

CLAUD. Thou thinkest I am in sport: I pray thee tell me truly how thou likest her.

BENE. Would you buy her, that you inquire after her?

CLAUD. Can the world buy such a jewel?

BENE. Yea, and a case to put it into. But speak you this with a sad brow, or do you play the flouting Jack, to tell us Cupid is a good hare-finder, and Vulcan a rare carpenter? Come, in what key shall a man take you, to go in the song?

CLAUD. In mine eyes she is the sweetest lady that ever I looked on.

BENE. I can yet see without spectacles and I see no such matter: there's her cousin, an she were not possessed with a fury, exceeds her as much in beauty as the first of May doth the last of December. But I hope you have no intent to turn husband, have you?

In this soliloquy, Benedick is being honest about his feelings towards Beatrice for the first time.

Act 2 Scene 3 (lines 240–266)

BENE.   *[advancing from the arbour]*
This can be no trick: the conference was sadly borne. They have the truth of this from Hero. They seem to pity the lady: it seems, her affections have their full bent. Love me! Why, it must be requited. I hear how I am censured: they say I will bear myself proudly, if I perceive the love come from her; they say too that she will rather die than give any sign of affection. I did never think to marry: I must not seem proud: happy are they that hear their detractions, and can put them to mending. They say the lady is fair: 'tis a truth, I can bear them witness; and virtuous: 'tis so, I cannot reprove it; and wise, but for loving me: by my troth, it is no addition to her wit, nor no great argument of her folly, for I will be horribly in love with her. I may chance have some odd quirks and remnants of wit broken on me, because I have railed so long against marriage; but doth not the appetite alter? A man loves the meat in his youth that he cannot endure in his age. Shall quips and sentences and these paper bullets of the brain awe a man from the career of his humour? No; the world must be peopled. When I said I would die a bachelor, I did not think I should live till I were married. Here comes Beatrice. By this day! She's a fair lady: I do spy some marks of love in her.

MUCH ADO ABOUT NOTHING

In order to work out what mark you would be awarded for your answer, do the following:

1   Read the **'Guidance on key features'** for each mark range.

2   Read carefully the **sample answers** for each mark range. These provide an example of the sorts of points that would be made by a student working within this mark range. Of course, you will not have written exactly the same remarks, but you should be able to tell if the **quality** of your writing is similar.

3   Now see if you can match *your* answer to a mark range. If you are unsure, ask someone you can trust – a relative, friend or teacher – to help you. Then, within the range, decide whether your answer deserves the top, middle or lowest mark. Is your answer a very good fit within the range (top mark), a reasonable fit (middle mark) or does it barely fit within it (lowest mark)?

4   Once you have decided what mark your answer would probably be given, look at **'How to improve your answer'**. This suggests what you need to do to improve your answer so that you can do better next time, and achieve a higher mark.

How well did you do?   *3–6 marks*

Guidance on key features

If your answer deserves a mark in this mark range:

- You will have made a clear distinction between what Benedick says about women and marriage in the first extract and the second.

- You will have related a little of the situation and included some relevant quotation.

Extract from a sample answer in this mark range

At the start Benedick is quite rude to Beatrice. He has met her before and knows that she has a sharp tongue. He calls her a "parrot-teacher". When Claudio is asking Benedick's opinion of Hero, the lady he admires, Benedick is not impressed, either by the lady or the idea of getting married. Later on, when Claudio, Don Pedro and Leonato are playing a trick on Benedick, making him think that Beatrice loves him, he seems to have changed his mind about getting married, "I have railed so long against marriage; but doth not the appetite alter?"

How to improve your answer

1   You need to be more explicit about how Benedick appears to the audience at both points in the play.

2   Your quotations are suitable but you should comment on what they tell you about Benedick.

3   Try to emphasise the great difference in Benedick's attitude in the two extracts.

How well did you do?   *7–10 marks*

Guidance on key features

If your answer deserves a mark in this mark range:

- You will have included plenty of detail to describe the situations. You will have illustrated them with quotations and commented on them.

- You will have included examples of what Benedick says and how he appears to the audience. You will have noted changes in his behaviour.

Extract from a sample answer in this mark range

Benedick starts off by calling Beatrice, "my dear Lady Disdain", which is not a very favourable greeting. He then seems conceited, saying, "I am loved of all ladies", but that he has not fallen in love with any of them, "truly, I love none".

When he turns to talk to Claudio, his attitude towards women is not any better, even though it is clear that his friend is in love with Hero. Benedick suggests she is not good-looking, even compared with Beatrice, "there's her cousin, and she were not possessed with a fury, exceeds her as much in beauty as the first of May doth the last of December".

In Act 2 Scene 3, when the lords play a trick on Benedick, to make him think Beatrice is in love with him, his arrogance seems to disappear and he is flattered. He says, "I will be horribly in love with her." He appears to the audience to be quite fickle as he has changed his mind so quickly.

How to improve your answer

1   You have started to draw comparisons between Benedick's appearances in the two scenes, but you need to emphasise the portrayal (how he seems) as well as what is said.

2   Concentrate on how extreme Benedick's opinions seem to be.

3   Develop the idea that because his change of mind is rapid, it is the more amusing.

How well did you do? *11–14 marks*

Guidance on key features

If your answer deserves a mark in this mark range:

- You will have detailed Benedick's opinions and attitudes using well-chosen quotations.

- You will have developed your character study of him in your commentary on the second extract, which provides a clear comparison with the first.

Extract from a sample answer in this mark range

At the beginning of the play, Benedick seems to be quite headstrong, having definite opinions on everything. He enjoys the banter with Beatrice, who is very much his equal. He appears to have a low opinion of her and of women in general. When Beatrice tells him she has no desire for a relationship, his response is, "some gentleman or other shall 'scape a scratched face".

Nor does he admit to Claudio that he appreciates the finer points of women; he pours cold water on Claudio's intention to woo Hero and teases him about getting married: "I hope you have no intent to turn husband, have you?"

However, these opinions of his are turned on their head when he is told, mischievously, that Beatrice is in love with him. He is flattered and pleased, and he revises his attitude towards her, "They say the lady is fair: 'tis a truth." He even turns immediately to thinking of marriage, "I have railed so long against marriage", though he knows he will be teased because of it, "Shall quips and sentences and these paper bullets of the brain awe a man from the career of his humour?"

How to improve your answer

1 Try to decide why Shakespeare portrays Benedick in two such different ways.

2 Analyse the language to make relevant comparisons.

3 Try to give an overview, integrating comment and textual reference.

How well did you do?   *15–18 marks*

Guidance on key features

If your answer deserves a mark in this mark range:

- You will have drawn out the main aspects of Benedick's behaviour in each extract.

- You will have compared them and commented on them, emphasising his complete turnaround in a very short space of time.

Extract from a sample answer in this mark range

In these two extracts, Benedick reveals two completely different sides to his character. In the first he is ebullient, arrogant and scathing about women: first of all in his conversation with Beatrice, where they engage in verbal jousting, each scoring points off the other with slick put-downs: "Beatrice. I wonder that you will still be talking, Signior Benedick: nobody marks you. Benedict. What! My dear Lady Disdain, are you yet living?"; secondly, in his discussion with Claudio about Hero, whom Claudio has chosen to woo:

> "Claudio. In my eyes she is the sweetest lady that ever I looked on.
> Benedict. I can see yet without spectacles and I see no such matter."

In the second extract, Benedick is duped by Don Pedro, Claudio and Leonato into believing that Beatrice loves him. He is clearly smitten by the idea and all his previously-voiced prejudices fall away in a revealing soliloquy.

You have 45 minutes to write your answer to the following task.

HENRY V

Act 4 Scene 1 (lines 133–188)
Act 5 Scene 2 (lines 133–176)

The play shows Henry to be a courageous and successful soldier. He is also skilful in argument and persuasion.

In the first extract, Henry is in disguise and is mixing with his soldiers before the Battle of Agincourt. He is arguing that the King is not responsible for the ways his soldiers may die.

In the second extract, Henry is persuading Catherine, the French King's daughter, to marry him, because he loves her.

Show how, in each scene, Henry is very clever in persuading people to his point of view.

(18 marks)

Reading extracts for
HENRY V

In this extract, Henry has disguised himself as a common soldier and is mixing with other soldiers very early in the morning before the battle of Agincourt. He wants to keep up their spirits and keep them loyal.

Act 4 Scene 1 (lines 133–188)

WILLIAMS   But if the cause be not good, the King himself hath a heavy reckoning to make, when all those legs and arms and heads chopped off in a battle shall join together at the latter day, and cry all, 'We died at such a place' – some swearing, some crying for a surgeon, some upon their wives left poor behind them, some upon the debts they owe, some upon their children rawly left. I am afeard there are few die well that die in a battle, for how can they charitably dispose of anything when blood is their argument? Now, if these men do not die well, it will be a black matter for the King that led them to it – who to disobey were against all proportion of subjection.

KING HENRY   So, if a son that is by his father sent about merchandise do sinfully miscarry upon the sea, the imputation of his wickedness, by your rule, should be imposed upon his father, that sent him. Or if a servant, under his master's command transporting a sum of money, be assailed by robbers, and die in many irreconciled iniquities, you may call the business of the master the author of the servant's damnation. But this is not so. The King is not bound to answer the particular endings of his soldiers, the father of his son, nor the master of his servant, for they purpose not their deaths when they propose their services. Besides, there is no king, be his cause never so spotless, if it come to the arbitrament of swords, can try it out with all unspotted soldiers. Some, peradventure, have on them the guilt of premeditated and contrived murder; some, of beguiling virgins with the broken seals of perjury; some, making the wars their bulwark, that have before gored the gentle bosom of peace with pillage and robbery. Now, if these men have defeated the law and outrun native punishment, though they can outstrip men, they have no wings to fly from God. War is his beadle. War is his vengeance. So that here men are punished for before-breach of the King's laws in now the King's quarrel. Where they feared the death, they have borne life away, and where they would be safe, they perish. Then if they die unprovided, no more is the King guilty of their damnation than he was before guilty of those impieties for the which they are now visited. Every subject's duty is the King's, but every subject's soul is his own. Therefore should every soldier in the wars do as every sick man in his bed: wash every mote out of his conscience. And dying so, death is to him advantage; or not dying, the time was blessedly lost wherein such preparation was gained. And in him that escapes, it were not sin to think that, making God so free an offer, he let him outlive that day to see his greatness and to teach others how they should prepare.

BATES 'Tis certain, every man that dies ill, the ill upon his own head. The King is not to answer it. I do not desire he should answer for me, and yet I determine to fight lustily for him.

In this scene, Henry is trying to persuade Catherine, (Kate), the French King's daughter, to marry him. He says he loves her, although it will be politically convenient for him to marry her.

Act 5 Scene 2 (lines 133–176)

KING HENRY Marry, if you would put me to verses, or to dance for your sake, Kate, why, you undid me; for the one I have neither words nor measure, and for the other I have no strength in measure – yet a reasonable measure in strength. If I could win a lady at leap-frog, or by vaulting into my saddle with my armour on my back, under the correction of bragging be it spoken, I should quickly leap into a wife. Or if I might buffet for my love, or bound my horse for her favours, I could lay on like a butcher, and sit like a jackanapes, never off. But before God, Kate, I cannot look greenly, nor gasp out my eloquence. Nor I have no cunning in protestation – only downright oaths, which I never use till urged, nor never break for urging. If thou canst love a fellow of this temper, Kate, whose face is not worth sunburning, that never looks in his glass for love of anything he sees there, let thine eye be thy cook. I speak to thee plain soldier: if thou canst love me for this, take me. If not, to say to thee that I shall die is true – but for thy love, by the Lord, no. Yet I love thee, too. And while thou livest, dear Kate, take a fellow of plain and uncoined constancy, for he perforce must do thee right, because he hath not the gift to woo in other places. For these fellows of infinite tongue, that can rhyme themselves into ladies' favours, they do always reason themselves out again. What! A speaker is but a prater, a rhyme is but a ballad; a good leg will fall, a straight back will stoop, a black beard will turn white, a curled pate will grow bald, a fair face will wither, a full eye will wax hollow, but a good heart, Kate, is the sun and the moon, or rather the sun and not the moon, for it shines bright and never changes, but keeps his course truly. If thou would have such a one, take me; and take me, take a soldier; tale a soldier, take a king. And what sayst thou then to my love? Speak, my fair – and fairly, I pray thee.

CATHERINE Is it possible dat I should love de *ennemi* of France?

KING HENRY No, it is not possible you should love the enemy of France, Kate. But in loving me, you should love the friend of France, for I love France so well that I will not part with a village of it. I will have it all mine, and Kate, when France is mine, and I am yours, then yours is France, and you are mine.

HENRY V

In order to work out what mark you would be awarded for your answer, do the following:

1 Read the **'Guidance on key features'** for each mark range.

2 Read carefully the **sample answers** for each mark range. These provide an example of the sorts of points that would be made by a student working within this mark range. Of course, you will not have written exactly the same remarks, but you should be able to tell if the **quality** of your writing is similar.

3 Now see if you can match *your* answer to a mark range. If you are unsure, ask someone you can trust – a relative, friend or teacher – to help you. Then, within the range, decide whether your answer deserves the top, middle or lowest mark. Is your answer a very good fit within the range (top mark), a reasonable fit (middle mark) or does it barely fit within it (lowest mark)?

4 Once you have decided what mark your answer would probably be given, look at **'How to improve your answer'**. This suggests what you need to do to improve your answer so that you can do better next time, and achieve a higher mark.

How well did you do?

3–6 marks

Guidance on key features

If your answer deserves a mark in this mark range:

- You will have summarised parts of the content of Henry's speeches and will have referred to the argument put forward by Williams, and to Bates' conclusion.

- You will not have commented on the persuasive skill of the speeches nor on the illustrations which form an important part of the argument. You will not have commented on Henry's view of his own character in the second scene.

Extract from a sample answer in this mark range

> Williams says that when soldiers have their legs and arms and heads chopped off in a battle, it is the King's fault because he sent them into battle. But Henry says that every soldier is different and they have all done wrong at some time, and so the King cannot be blamed for what that soldier has done and how God deals with him after he has died. Bates agrees with this.
>
> When he is talking to Kate, Henry says that he cannot dance for her sake, or tell verses, and he is not a good speaker, as he cannot gasp out any eloquence. He does not think he is good-looking. But he says that all good-looking men will grow old and white and bald. He asks Kate if she will have him as a plain soldier and if she will marry him now he is the King of France and loves her with a good heart.

How to improve your answer

1. Try to deal with the whole speech in each extract, and not just bits of the speeches.

2. The question is about Henry's skill in persuasion, and so state this at the beginning and point out that the examples he gives show his skill. Refer to his own illustrations as you make your points.

3. Give short quotations from the speeches to show how your points are relevant to the question, and use inverted commas round the quotations.

How well did you do?

7–10 marks

Guidance on key features

If your answer deserves a mark in this mark range:

- You will have given more detail from the text and this detail will have been organised so that it is clearly relevant to the question.

- You will have included quotations and you will have referred to many of the illustrations in the argument that Henry himself uses.

- You will have included the points of view of Williams and Bates and you will have given some account of Henry's witty reply to Catherine's question about an enemy of France.

Extract from a sample answer in this mark range

When Williams argues that the King is responsible for all the horrible, painful deaths of all the soldiers killed in battle because he commanded them to fight, Henry has a clever and persuasive answer which denies this and defends the King. He says that if a father sends his son on a journey, or if a servant is given a commercial task by his master, and if the son or the servant come to grief because of their own silly or wicked ways, the father or master cannot be blamed for that silliness or wickedness. So, every soldier is an individual who may be good or evil or weak or foolish, and the King is not responsible for all this. Bates agrees with this: "Every man that dies ill, the ill upon his own head. The King is not to answer it."

Catherine knows quite well how good a soldier Henry is, but as he tries to get her to marry him, he points out that he does not have skill in eloquence or dancing: "I have neither words nor measure". So he turns his plain and direct nature to his own advantage, admitting he is not handsome or fashionable, but loves her with a "good heart". He says he loves France as well, and now owns it, so that if she will be his, then she will also own France and him.

How to improve your answer

1   This answer traces the arguments used by Henry. The answer is coherently organised but the quality needs to be improved by showing how Henry handles these arguments with persuasive cleverness.

2   Analyse how Henry brings God into the situation, as he often does, to show that his cause is right.

3   Examine Henry's view of his own character, and show how he turns his shortcomings to his own advantage.

How well did you do?

11–14 marks

Guidance on key features

If your answer deserves a mark in this mark range:

- You will have given a careful analysis of Henry's skill in argument and his power of persuasion.
- You will have considered how effective the illustrations of the father and master are for Henry's arguments.
- You will also have considered the reason why Henry introduces into his argument the idea of God's judgment.
- You will have pointed out the cleverness of Henry's pretending to be a "plain soldier" with no literary or courtly accomplishments and no rhetorical ability, while in truth he is a clever and skilful orator.

Extract from a sample answer in this mark range

At first sight, Williams's statement that when men meet gruesome deaths in battle it must be the king's responsibility because he sent them to fight, seems a sound argument. However, by using the illustrations of a father sending his son and a merchant sending his servant on expeditions, Henry seems to change the way of looking at the problem. It is true that the father or merchant cannot be responsible for the way the son or servant conduct themselves, and so who is to blame for what happens to them? Henry also distinguishes between public duty and private behaviour and gives the argument a religious dimension by saying that every person is responsible to God for their behaviour. The illustrations and this distinction convince Bates that Henry is right.

When Henry is speaking to Catherine, he is keen to present himself as a "plain soldier", without the courtly skills of rhetoric or dancing or poetry. He dismisses these and also says that any physical attributes will grow old and feeble. So, while pretending to be plain and simple, in fact he manipulates his argument cleverly and persuasively, even to the point of saying he conquered France because he loved it, and if Catherine marries him, she will also own it.

How to improve your answer

1   This answer has made all the relevant points in a well-organised way, but now needs to comment on the quality of the argument and illustrations: the task is to "Show how … Henry is very clever in persuading people…".

2   Search for a short quotation which exactly expresses the points Henry is making to the soldiers, and work it into the text of your answer.

3   Try to select the best language of your own, which expresses your thoughts and ideas in a succinct way, so that your answer clearly belongs to the top mark range.

How well did you do?

15–18 marks

Guidance on key features

If your answer deserves a mark in this mark range:

- You will have commented on the quality of Henry's argument and persuasive speech.
- You will have analysed his technique, commenting on the quality of the illustrations that he uses within his argument.
- You will have used, and commented on, brief quotations which you will have selected in such a way as to encapsulate the essence of his argument.
- Your ideas will have been developed and structured with succinct and thoughtful expression.

Extract from a sample answer in this mark range

Williams's graphic description of the terrible carnage of warfare only emphasises how heavy is the responsibility the King bears for it, because it was he who sent the soldiers into battle to die in agony. Henry counters this with the analogy of a father sending his son on an enterprise in which he behaves badly, and a merchant sending a servant who is killed on his master's business. These two illustrations relate to family life and daily business and so would have been well understood by Henry's audience, the common soldiers. The illustrations are effective in showing that the problem of responsibility is far more complicated than Williams says it is, because factors of character are relevant.

This naturally introduces the argument about a person's relationship to God as well as the King, as a distinction between public duty and private behaviour is made. "Every subject's duty is the King's, but every subject's soul is his own," says Henry. Henry had sought the blessing of the church before he started his war, and at that time, religion was very influential in the way men thought. The course of this argument therefore convinces Bates that Henry is right, and he will "determine to fight lustily for him".

Henry shows his persuasive cleverness as he proposes marriage to Catherine by adopting a position as a "plain soldier" – that is, simple, direct and honest, without the sophistication that Catherine would have been familiar with in her father's court. "I have neither words nor measure," he says, in order to recite poetry or dance for her. He says "I cannot… gasp out my eloquence," and yet this is a skilful argument he adopts, as it shows him to be modest and trustworthy, "a fellow of plain and uncoined constancy". Clever people, he argues, will always think of excuses for being unfaithful, and however handsome they might be, eventually "a fair face will wither, a full eye will wax hollow". When she asks how she could love an enemy of France, he turns this to his own advantage, saying he conquered France because he loved it, and if she would have him, she would have France, too. Henry can overcome any difficulty to make his argument convincing, and it is eventually successful.